East of the Sun, West of the Moon

By
BRIAN KRAL

Dramatic Publishing Company
Woodstock, Illinois ● Australia ● New Zealand ● South Africa

*** NOTICE ***

The amateur and stock acting rights to this work are controlled exclusively by THE DRAMATIC PUBLISHING COMPANY, INC., without whose permission in writing no performance of it may be given. Royalty must be paid every time a play is performed whether or not it is presented for profit and whether or not admission is charged. A play is performed any time it is acted before an audience. Current royalty rates, applications and restrictions may be found at our website: www.dramaticpublishing.com, or we may be contacted by mail at: THE DRAMATIC PUBLISHING COMPANY, INC., 311 Washington St., Woodstock, IL 60098.

COPYRIGHT LAW GIVES THE AUTHOR OR THE AUTHOR'S AGENT THE EXCLUSIVE RIGHT TO MAKE COPIES. This law provides authors with a fair return for their creative efforts. Authors earn their living from the royalties they receive from book sales and from the performance of their work. Conscientious observance of copyright law is not only ethical, it encourages authors to continue their creative work. This work is fully protected by copyright. No alterations, deletions or substitutions may be made in the work without the prior written consent of the publisher. No part of this work may be reproduced or transmitted in any form or by any means, electronic or mechanical, including photocopy, recording, videotape, film, or any information storage and retrieval system, without permission in writing from the publisher. It may not be performed either by professionals or amateurs without payment of royalty. All rights, including, but not limited to, the professional, motion picture, radio, television, videotape, foreign language, tabloid, recitation, lecturing, publication and reading, are reserved.

> For performance of any songs, music and recordings mentioned in this play which are in copyright, the permission of the copyright owners must be obtained or other songs and recordings in the public domain substituted.

© 1987 by
ANCHORAGE PRESS, INC.

Printed in the United States of America
All Rights Reserved
(EAST OF THE SUN, WEST OF THE MOON)

ISBN: 978-0-87602-273-3

IMPORTANT BILLING AND CREDIT REQUIREMENTS

All producers of the play *must* give credit to the author of the play in all programs distributed in connection with performances of the play and in all instances in which the title of the play appears for purposes of advertising, publicizing or otherwise exploiting the play and/or a production. The name of the author *must* also appear on a separate line, on which no other name appears, immediately following the title, and *must* appear in size of type not less than fifty percent (50%) the size of the title type. Biographical information on the author, if included in the playbook, may be used in all programs. *In all programs this notice must appear:*

"Produced by special arrangement with
THE DRAMATIC PUBLISHING COMPANY, INC., of Woodstock, Illinois."

Thank You:
TO FRITZ LEIBER
for odd folk, other worlds,
and a lasting love of Fantasy;
AND TO GAYLE CORNELISON,
another brooding Scandinavian
with a quiet propensity to dream.

EAST OF THE SUN was written as partial fulfillment of the MFA degree at Arizona State, with residency made possible through special arrangement between California Young People's Theatre and the Rainbow Company Children's Theatre. EAST OF THE SUN was first performed by California Young People's Theatre, May 11, 1983, at the Sunnyvale Community Center. It was produced by executive director Gayle Cornelison, and directed by Scott Williams, with the following actors:

Karin .... Mary Gibboney

Mother, and Troll
    Princess .... Shannon Edwards

Peder, and
    Karin's Father .... Chuck Rounds

Troll Queen, and
    South Wind .... Rachel LePell

1st Hag, North Wind,
    and Stone Figure .... Richard Plombon

2nd Hag, East Wind,
    and Horick .... Chuck Abernathy

3rd Hag, West Wind,
    and Stone Figure .... Dorien Wilson

Costumes were by Pam Cornelison, Sets and lights by Ralph J. Ryan, with Technical Direction by Anders Bolang. The production Stage Manager was Duncan Graham.

The play was selected for the Children's Theatre Association's "Unpublished Play Listing" and was able to evolve into the present draft after subsequent productions with the following producers and directors: Jane Campbell and John Kauffman at Honolulu Theater for Youth; Johnny Saldana and Rick Atkins at Arizona State University; and Brian Strom (of all people) with the Rainbow Company in Las Vegas. Each production, through the care and support of talented production staff, was instrumental in polishing the play. They deserve the author's thanks and recognition.

Characters (in order of appearance):

Karin, a young girl
Her Mother
Peder, the White Bear
An Older Woman, the Troll Queen
A Younger Woman, the Troll Princess
The First Hag
The Second Hag
The Third Hag
Karin's Father, a spectral figure
The East Wind
The West Wind
The South Wind
The North Wind
Horick, a Troll attendant
First Stone Figure
Second Stone Figure

Time and Place:

Castles, cottages, and the frozen wilderness of Old Norway after the advent of Christianity.

By doubling actors in multiple roles, a great economy in cast size can be achieved. The only character that cannot be doubled is Karin.

The play is divided into three acts. The first act represents the visible world, in which magic and religion co-exist, mysteriously, in the shadows. At the conclusion of the act, the familiar world is stripped away, showing the Trolls as they are. The second act shows a desolate wilderness, where characters and incidents are influenced by Karin's psychological and emotional struggle. The troll kingdom is made up of mismatched parts of the real world. The Trolls exaggerate the worst of human nature and mock Christian behavior, with more sympathetic human values as counterpoint. These three acts vary in tone and style; a compelling dramatic throughline must be established and maintained for the audience to accompany Karin on her journey through these changing states. The play can be performed without intermission.

EAST OF THE SUN, WEST OF THE MOON

Scene One

A room in a Norwegian home. Furnishings are of wood, but there are not many and those that are there are simple. Karin, a young woman, stands on a stool, while her mother kneels below her, pinning the hem of a lovely wedding gown.

MOTHER: Hold still. I'm almost finished.

(Karin shifts on the stool, trying to look at the gown.)

KARIN: Ow! You stuck me.

MOTHER: Yes, and I'll do it again if you don't stop squirming.

(She stands, steps around to see the back.)

KARIN: *(to herself)*
You did it on purpose.

(Her mother spanks her once with the back of her hand.)

MOTHER: Stand up straight so I can see how it looks.

(She studies it, nods.)

It's good. Ten maidens' hands couldn't have done as well. Take it off, and I'll finish the stitching.

(She goes to a table, lays out her materials. Karin steps down, admiring the gown.)

KARIN: It isn't fair.

MOTHER: What's that?

KARIN: That you make such clothes for other people,—

MOTHER: *(threading her needle)*
They pay for them.

KARIN: *(still admiring the gown)*
—while I wear the same things year in and year out.

(Her mother again spanks her.)

MOTHER: Hurry up, or I'll be at this all evening.

(*Karin removes the gown. Beneath it she wears a simple cloth shift. Her mother takes the gown, and begins sewing the hem.*)

KARIN: Why are you so mean to me?

MOTHER: *(sewing)*
I'm not. I have work to get done.

KARIN: You treat me like I wasn't yours.

MOTHER: Don't talk nonsense.

KARIN: Like I was some monster baby the trolls left in your cradle.

MOTHER: Stop that! It's bad luck to mention the trolls. Especially at night.

KARIN: Our luck couldn't be any worse.

MOTHER: *(resuming her sewing)*
Hush, now. You'll wake your father. And you know he needs his rest.

KARIN: I have needs too. But who cares about those? Who cares for the needs of an orphan?

MOTHER: You're not an orphan, it's just your age. I don't know why but sooner or later all girls feel unloved by their mothers.

KARIN: Not all get sent away.

(*Pause.*)

MOTHER: You don't have to go.

KARIN: No, I could stay and starve and the family would suffer. Unless I worked. I could bring in enough money to help you with father!

MOTHER: What could you do?

KARIN: I do housework, don't I?

MOTHER: *(gently chiding)*
Sometimes. But who'd pay for that?

KARIN: *(dejected again, she touches the gown)*
You're right, I clean like a troll—everything I touch gets dirtier. I'll go. And maybe I'll have beautiful dresses like this, all for myself.

MOTHER: *(finishing her work)*
Pack it away. They'll come for it tomorrow.
(Karin takes the gown, to wrap it in cloth.)
I hope you will have many dresses, Karin. And that you'll be...happy.

KARIN: That's a hard word to say, huh? I know you haven't had much to be happy about. But I will, you'll see. You won't find me making dresses for other people's weddings!
(She carelessly drops the bundle on the table, but her mother ignores her. Pause.)
What is it made Papa so sick?

MOTHER: Only God knows. And He has his reasons.

KARIN: You still have faith? After everything?

MOTHER: He's brought you salvation, hasn't He? Why are you smirking?

KARIN: Nowhere in my catechism did the Pastor have a White Bear as salvation.

MOTHER: "Tender mercies, God's good grace, Smile in any form He takes." Besides, it wasn't a bear.

KARIN: That's what the neighbors said.

MOTHER: They only spy so they'll have something to whisper; they didn't speak to him.

KARIN: Him!

MOTHER: Yes, him. He looks like a bear, but he talks like a man.

KARIN: I'd go with him anyway, Mother, even if he was a dragon! First, because you promised...but also because he claims a great fortune! I am relieved he talks, though. Oh! Maybe he's a handsome landowner, hexed by the trolls!

MOTHER: Stop it! And at this hour.

(She makes a superstitious gesture, to protect against the trolls—spitting in her palm, kissing an amulet, etc. Karin laughs.)

You shouldn't make fun of such things.

KARIN: Why? Surely with "God's good graces"—

MOTHER: *(seriously)*

Even in a good world there's evil enough to get underfoot. And it may be waiting for you!

(Pause. Karin repeats the protective gesture her mother had used, suddenly frightened. There is a heavy knock on the door. Karin jumps, startled. She looks to her mother.)

MOTHER: Yes, it's him. You'd better get your things.

(Karin exits, as her mother goes to let the visitor in. Outside, in the dim light, stands the tall White Bear. She stands aside to admit him, but he remains on the threshold, wrapped in shadow. Wind whistles behind him.)

WHITE BEAR: Good evening to you. Is your daughter willing to go?

MOTHER: *(uneasy)*

Yes. She's just...putting on her cloak.

WHITE BEAR: *(handing her a leather pouch)*

Here is your payment. With each cycle of the moon I'll deliver another, for every month of the year she is to stay with me.

(The mother has opened the pouch and holds a handful of gold coins. She drops them back.)

MOTHER: Bless you!

WHITE BEAR: As promised, you'll be as rich as you are now poor.

MOTHER: And her?

WHITE BEAR: She'll be taken care of.

MOTHER: You'll be...kind to her?

WHITE BEAR: She's to be my companion—my friend. She'll have every consideration.

MOTHER: Thank you.

(*Karin enters, sees the White Bear in the doorway, and tenses visibly. Her mother crosses to her, trying to appear calm.*)
You have your hood up?
(*Adjusting it around Karin's face.*)
Good.

WHITE BEAR: Pull it close. The wind is cruel tonight.

(*Karin stands still, staring at the large bear. Her mother runs to the table, grabbing up the bundle.*)

MOTHER: Here. I want you to take this with you.

(*She places the bundle in Karin's hands.*)

KARIN: But, mother, I—

MOTHER: I'll make another. I'll tell them I had the wrong material, they'll understand.

KARIN: (*forcefully*)
What do I need with a wedding dress?

(*Pause. Her mother looks at her, then again adusts her hood, sweeping the hair from Karin's face.*)

MOTHER: Someday you will. Someday.

(*Karin walks past her mother, to the door. Her mother runs to a small cache of food.*)
And, here. This bread and cheese will be welcome.

(*She hands it to Karin, steps back into the room, clutching her shawl around her throat.*)

WHITE BEAR: (*offering her a hand up*)
Climb onto my back. And hold tight to my shaggy coat.

(*She tucks the food and her bundle under her arm, climbing onto his back.*)

There's nothing to fear.

(*He carries her slowly out of the light of the doorway into the darkness.*)

MOTHER: *(as Karin disappears from view)*
> Don't be bitter, Karin, towards God or me.
>
> *(She runs to the open doorway.)*
>
> Turn your heart to Christian thoughts and be **thankful** you're being delivered from this.
>
> *(Calling out into the night.)*
>
> Be thankful!
>
> *(The wind grows louder.)*

Scene Two

The mountains at night. Karin and the White Bear move in and out of view as he carries her through the shadows. Wind whistles around them.

KARIN: *(holding on to his coat)*
> I can't see a thing. Where are we headed?

WHITE BEAR: To my castle.
> *(Pause. He runs with a predictable rhythm. The long journey through the mountains is made by mixing the dialogue in with the constant motion of running. Even when they speak, the bear continues running evenly.)*

KARIN: Aren't you tired? Perhaps we could rest?

WHITE BEAR: I'm colder than I am tired. We'll go on.
> *(Pause. Each piece of conversation finds them in a new location, but the rhythm of the running continues unchanged.)*

KARIN: Couldn't we slow down?...My legs are stiff and my fingers are freezing—how must you feel?

WHITE BEAR: Impatient to be home. Hold tighter.
> *(Pause. The wind quiets, and Karin sags wearily against the bear's back but she maintains her hold on his coat as he continues running.)*

KARIN: Can't you tell me something about yourself?
> *(She yawns.)*
>
> Are you really a bear?

WHITE BEAR: You ask too many questions.

> *(He slows down, then stops.)*
> And besides, . .we're here.
> *(Revealed within the forested mountains is the palatial bed chamber of the White Bear's castle.)*
> We've arrived.
> *(Karin has fallen asleep; she slowly slides off his back onto the ground, and into a curled up, sleeping position. The White Bear lifts her gently, and carries her into the castle. The chamber glows hazily from candlelight. Within the chamber, he lowers her slowly onto a large, luxurious bed, with flowing quilt and billowing canopy. Karin's bundle slips from her arms, and two shadowy women appear—one young, the other older—to whisk the bundle from the floor and to arrange Karin on the bed. The White Bear pulls a heavy dividing curtain forward, separating the two sides of the bed. He crosses to the far side of the bed, away from Karin.)*

YOUNG WOMAN: *(whispering)*
> She came, after all. What will we do?

OLDER WOMAN: *(whispering)*
> Nothing to do. Wait and see.
> *(The two women hurry quietly to the White Bear. They ceremoniously remove the heavy coat and head that give him the appearance of a bear, showing him to be a handsome, well-dressed young man, in elegant breeches and a loose-fitting white nightshirt. On the other side of the curtain, Karin awakens and sits up, running her hand over the soft quilt. The two women carry the bear's coat out of view. The young man—Peder—sits on his side of the curtain, and speaks quietly to Karin.)*

PEDER: Are you awake?

KARIN: *(leaning into the curtain)*
> Do you truly have a castle?

PEDER: Just as you see.

KARIN: *(sitting back, to look again)*
> Then I guess I'm awake.

PEDER: Are you impressed?

(Karin nods her head, looking around—then realizes he cannot see her.)

KARIN: I mean, Yes. Yes, I am. It's wonderful.

PEDER: There's much more than this room. But you can see that tomorrow. Beside the bed is a silver bell. Ring it, and anything you wish will be yours—

(Her hand immediately reaches for it.)

Tomorrow! For now, we'll both get some rest.

KARIN: *(leaning into the curtain)*

Not yet! Who are you? Why did you bring me here?

PEDER: I'll tell you my name: Peder. But that's all. Except for this warning: you must never try to see what I look like asleep.

KARIN: Asleep? What do you mean?

PEDER: Nothing. Be satisfied that, tomorrow, when you see me, I'll be just as you remember: a large white bear, with shaggy, matted coat.

(Pause.)

KARIN: And now?. . .Peder?

(Pause. The two women have reappeared.)

PEDER: *(suddenly frightened)*

You mustn't ask! Go to sleep!

(He turns away from the curtain, covering himself with the quilt. Karin waits, then slowly lies down on her side of the curtain. The two women remain in the shadows, dimly lit.)

OLDER WOMAN: *(whispering)*

Wait and see.

Scene Three

The bedchamber of Peder's castle, the following morning. Peder has gone, and sunlight filters into the room through drapes, but Karin is still asleep. The younger woman of the previous night is slowly sweeping with an old broom. She can be seen now to be dressed in dreary clothes, to appear to be a servant, with a dark shawl to cover her head. Karin awakens, sits up, and stretches luxuriously, until a sudden twinge of pain makes her curl up.

KARIN: Oh! I have a charly-horse.

(The woman ignores Karin, continues sweeping.)

Can you get those from riding a bear?

(The woman ignores her. Karin watches her, then surreptitiously lifts the dividing curtain to peek underneath. When she sees he isn't there, she draws it back altogether.)

Where is he?

YOUNGER WOMAN: *(sweeping)*
Gone.

(She uses a deep voice to sound more gruff.)

KARIN: Where to?

YOUNGER WOMAN: Don't know.

(Pause. She continues sweeping slowly. Karin swings her legs off the bed, cringes again and rubs her leg. She reaches out to ring the silver bell.)

Don't bother.

(Younger woman drops her broom, strides off. She returns with a breakfast tray, sets it on the bed with a clatter, returns to her sweeping.)

KARIN: *(staring at the tray)*
He was right.

(She takes a piece of toast, nibbles on it.)

What do you do here?

(Younger woman looks at Karin, continues sweeping. Karin finishes her toast.)

When will he be back?

(Woman continues to ignore her. Cheerily:)

You have an interesting nose. But it's so long.

(Woman stops, looks at Karin, who smiles.)

YOUNGER WOMAN: You'll see him at dinner.

KARIN: *(picking up a delicate cup)*
Thank you.

(Karin reaches down, but her bundle is missing.)

Did you see my dress?

(Younger woman walks to a curtained area, draws them back to reveal several hanging dresses, returns to her sweeping. Karin goes to them, holding up several.)

They're wonderful! But I had a wedding dress I brought with me.

YOUNGER WOMAN: *(eyeing her)*
A wedding dress? Where'd you get it?

KARIN: *(looking through the dresses)*
My mother made it. She'd do practically anything for me.
(Pause. The woman resumes sweeping.)
Which do you think I should wear for—
(Suddenly realizing.)
Dinner? What do bears eat?

YOUNGER WOMAN: *(maliciously)*
People, mostly. Sometimes little girls. With tiny noses.
(Karin drops the dress she's holding.)

KARIN: Aren't they...more partial...to fish?

YOUNGER WOMAN: Sure they are. **Raw** fish. Bones and all. So they're...crunchy.

KARIN: *(slowly overcoming her distaste)*
I suppose that's better than people.

YOUNGER WOMAN: If you wanted to go home, though,—

KARIN: No, I'll be fine.

YOUNGER WOMAN: *(disappointed)*
Suit yourself.

KARIN: *(picking up the fallen dress)*
Anyway, I couldn't go home if I wanted to. I've got to stay.
(Brightening up.)

And who **wouldn't** want to be in a beautiful castle; where everything you wish for is yours, from breakfast in bed to glittering gowns! I'd be a **fool** to leave now.

(She starts out, then stops, piously.)

Besides. To stay is the Christian thing to do, isn't it?

(She smiles and exits, carrying a dress.)

YOUNGER WOMAN: *(glaring after her)*
I wouldn't know.

(She drops the broom, and recovers the bundle where she had hidden it the night before. Lights slowly fade on the bedchamber.)

Scene Four

Afternoon of the same day, in the courtyard of Peder's castle. Birds can be heard singing cheerily, until the young woman from the previous scene appears, running in stealthily with Karin's bundle. She sets it down, kneels, and begins to unwrap it. A shrill bird whistle replaces the cheerful singing.

YOUNG WOMAN: *(angrily; evilly)*
Shoo!

(The birds squawk, flap off noisily. She tosses her nose at them contemptuously, then finishes with her unwrapping.)

Ohhh!

(She holds up the wedding gown, entranced. The older woman enters, carrying a broom.)

OLDER WOMAN: What are you doing?

(Younger woman jumps, startled, concealing the gown.)

Do you want to ruin everything?

(Younger woman shakes her head.)

Put that back before—

KARIN: *(calling as she enters courtyard)*
Hello?

(Both women jump. The younger one stands in front of the bundle to hide it.)

I thought I heard voices. I was just looking for a package I'd brought with me from home, and hoped you might have. . .

(She notices the younger woman is standing very rigidly, her eyes wide, face neutral.)

Is something wrong with her?

OLDER WOMAN: That's my daughter. She doesn't have the capacity to speak.

(The younger woman looks at the older one, narrows her eyes angrily.)

KARIN: *(sympathetically)*

Really?

OLDER WOMAN: *(to the younger one)*

Ever since she was a child. Hasn't uttered a sound.

(Younger woman rolls her eyes to the sky, resigns herself and turns back to face Karin.)

KARIN: How awful.

(Whispering to older woman.)

She does have a tongue, doesn't she?

OLDER WOMAN: *(to younger)*

Show her.

(Younger woman opens her mouth, hanging out her tongue.)

See? As good as the day she was made.

(She remains with tongue out. Sweetly:)

You can close your mouth now, dear.

(The older woman pushes up on her chin, causing the younger woman to bite her tongue painfully.)

KARIN: How odd. She looks just like the girl I spoke with this morning.

OLDER WOMAN: That was. . .my other daughter.

KARIN: *(studying her more closely)*

Oh yes. I see the difference. This one's nose is much longer.

(Karin steps away innocently, with the younger woman fuming. The older one restrains her, as Karin looks around the courtyard and surrounding foliage.)

Anyway, you haven't seen a small bundle? Wrapped in cloth? I don't know where it could have gone.

OLDER WOMAN: *(as the younger shakes her head)*
   As a matter of fact, . . .
   (Younger huffs, pouts, crossing her arms.)
   . . .my daughter did find it—and was just returning it to you. Weren't you, dear?
   (Begrudgingly, the younger woman recovers the bundle, holds it out to Karin.)
   She thought it was laundry that needed washing.

KARIN: Hardly. This dress has never been worn.

OLDER WOMAN: So we saw. Where did you get such a lovely gown?

YOUNGER WOMAN: *(whispering)*
   Her mother made it.
   (Older woman brings the tip of the broom-handle down on the other's foot. She reacts silently to the pain, hopping on other foot.)

OLDER WOMAN: *(sweetly)*
   Did she? I mean,—Did your mother make it?

KARIN: Yes. How did you know?

OLDER WOMAN: Mothers can tell such things.

KARIN: *(holding up the gown to model it)*
   Well, mine loves me very much. She picked out each of the pearls in its hem especially for me.

OLDER WOMAN: How did you bring yourself to leave that. . .loving mother?

KARIN: *(becoming serious; folding the gown)*
   It was the right thing to do, we decided—out of goodwill.
   (She drops the gown onto its wrapping.)
   The bear. . . .He looked so lonely.
   (Slight pause.)
   Do you think he's really a bear?
   (Both women freeze, shifting their full attention to Karin.)

OLDER WOMAN: *(cautiously)*
   What else could he be?

KARIN: I don't know, he might be anything, if you believe such things—even a troll!
   (The two women look at one another, suddenly on guard.)

OLDER WOMAN: But, if he were a troll, . . .how could he walk around during the day? Don't all trolls turn to stone in the sun?

KARIN: Not if they've taken on some other shape, I'll bet. Like a bear, for instance. Then they could walk around causing all sorts of mischief.

OLDER WOMAN: *(edging towards other woman)*
   Is that so?

KARIN: It's possible. And he'd turn back into a troll at night!

OLDER WOMAN: Fancy that.

KARIN: And if he were a troll,—Why I'd **never** want to know what he looked like.
   (Younger one strikes her palm against her forehead.)
   It would be simply too dreadful.

OLDER WOMAN: I can see that. . . .But what if he were some other thing. Other than a troll. Wouldn't you be. . .curious. . .then?

KARIN: Like what?

OLDER WOMAN: I don't know, really. Something else. Like a. . . handsome young man?

KARIN: What makes you think he's handsome?

OLDER WOMAN: I don't, necessarily, I'm saying he might be.
   (Slight pause.)
   What do you think, . . .Karin?

KARIN: How did you know my—
   (Peder charges in, in the shape of the bear, frightening the two women and sending them scattering.)

PEDER: *(bellowing)*
> What are you doing out here?

KARIN: *(startled by the sudden appearance)*
> Oh! I was just . . .introducing myself to your servants.

PEDER: Is that what they said they were?

OLDER WOMAN: *(composed)*
> No, she's a clever girl. She guessed it all on her own.
> *(She sweeps deliberately, smiling at Peder, who glowers at the two women.)*

KARIN: *(whispering politely)*
> The daughter's a bit strange. But I like the older lady quite a lot. What are their names.

PEDER: *(watching them, suspiciously)*
> Why don't you ask them?
> *(Peder steps back, his anger subsiding, as Karin looks to the two women.)*

OLDER WOMAN: Her name is. . .Ermengarde.
> *(The younger's mouth drops open, outraged.)*
> And you can call me "Mama." Just like your own sweet mother.
> *(Peder takes Karin roughly by the arm, pulling her aside.)*

PEDER: *(low and intense)*
> Listen to me, or you'll bring us both bad luck! You must talk to no one alone, and accept no advice, for as long as you're here, do you understand? Otherwise—
> *(He is interrupted by the sharp rap of the wooden broomhandle on hard ground. He stops, releases his hold on Karin's arm. She steps back a pace, rubbing her shoulder. To her:)*
> You're frightened of me aren't you. I didn't mean you to be.

KARIN: You hurt my arm. That's all.

PEDER: I'm sorry. Forgive me.

KARIN: *(still rubbing the shoulder)*
All right.

(Pause. Peder looks past her to the two women; the older one moves away, presumably sweeping, but without conviction.)

PEDER: Actually, I don't mind you being in the courtyard. Considering what it cost me. But you must remember what I said! *(She flinches, pulling back as he reaches for her; slight pause.)*

KARIN: I will.

PEDER: Fine. . . .But that's not why I came out. You've been told about dinner? That we'll be eating together?

KARIN: Yes.

PEDER: Good.
(To older woman:)
And you'll see to it there's something she likes?

OLDER WOMAN: Certainly, . . .sir.
(Pause.)

PEDER: All right, then. At dinner.
(He hesitates, then goes. Karin watches.)

KARIN: *(resuming the rubbing of her shoulder)*
I believe he is a bear. He almost tore it right out of its socket.

OLDER WOMAN: Remember what you said earlier, though. Don't forget he might be—

KARIN: *(interrupting)*
No. I'll. . .remember.
(She hastily picks up her gown and wrapping.)
I'd better—hang up my dress now. Good-bye.
(She exits quickly.)

YOUNGER WOMAN: The little twit! Why didn't you tell her everything? So we could be rid of her!

OLDER WOMAN: *(very calmly)*
> Everything will be told in its time, my darling, we're not finished yet. I want her to know just enough to make her curious—without becoming suspicious.
> *(She smiles.)*
> Trust your mother, . . . "Ermengarde."
> *(The older woman exits, carrying the broom.)*

YOUNGER WOMAN: *(twisting her face)*
> Ermengarde?
> *(A shiver runs through her, and she hurries off after her mother.)*

Scene Five

That evening, in the bedchamber. A small table and two chairs have been added, where Peder and Karin are finishing their dinner.

PEDER: *(in the shape of the bear)*
> How was it?

KARIN: *(eating)*
> Very good!
> *(Leaning over to whisper, conspiratorially.)*
> Even better than my mother made it!

PEDER: *(also whispering, to play along)*
> I hoped it would be!
> *(Speaking in his natural voice.)*
> Can I get you anything else?

KARIN: *(eating the last of it)*
> Uh-uh! I'm stuffed. It was wonderful.
> *(She smiles, then thinks of him across the table.)*
> But it must have been terrible for you.

PEDER: Why?

KARIN: Well, . . .it wasn't fish.

PEDER: *(laughing)*
Thank God!

KARIN: But I thought you liked fish.

PEDER: Oh no! When I was younger I couldn't even bring myself to look at a pickled herring, let alone eat it like my father. He'd put them on little crackers and pop them into his mouth. Just like chestnuts.

KARIN: I didn't know bears ate pickled herring.
(Peder laughs again, louder.)
Why are you laughing? Did I say something stupid?

PEDER: No. You're charming. I was laughing. . .because I'm enjoying myself.
(He reaches out his hand to hers, but then withdraws it.)
I wish I could be honest with you, and tell you why you're here.
(The two women have appeared in the background, standing in the shadows, ominously.)
But you'll have to be patient. And remember my warning. Now, . . .to bed.
(Karin tries to stop him, but Peder has already gone off to his side of the bed. He pulls the curtain across brusquely, as the older woman comes down to remove his chair.)

OLDER WOMAN: *(whispering)*
What do you say now?
(She hurries off before Karin can answer. Karin goes to her side, curious. On the other side, the younger woman helps Peder off with his bear fur.)

KARIN: Peder? What was your father like?

PEDER: *(thinking)*
He was. . .a great burly bear of a man.

KARIN: But he was a man?
(Pause.)

PEDER: You ask too many questions for this late at night. Go to sleep, before you bring us bad luck.

(He lies down on his side, as the woman approaches Karin again from the darkness.)

OLDER WOMAN: *(whispering)*
Do you still think he's a troll?

KARIN: *(whispering)*
I can't be sure!

OLDER WOMAN: *(sweeping down to other chair)*
Test him!
(She whisks off the chair as the younger takes the table. Karin thinks, considering.)

KARIN: Oh! Did you hear it?

PEDER: What?

KARIN: Quick! Give me your hand, I'm frightened!
(Without thinking, he reaches around front. Karin grabs his hand, sees that it's human.)

PEDER: You're quiet. Are you all right?

KARIN: Yes, it's. . .your hand is. . .so strong. Thank you. I feel better.
(He slowly pulls his hand back.)

PEDER: And the sound?

KARIN: It's gone. A bad dream.

(Pause.)

You may not believe it, but this isn't the first time I've slept in the same room as a man. And I don't mean my father, when I was a little girl.

PEDER: *(half asleep)*
You still are a little girl.

KARIN: *(ignoring it)*

At my grandmother's farm, they didn't think so. When a girl—a young lady—reaches her confirmation, she's treated like an adult. The harvest I worked there they let all the boys and girls sleep in the same hall. Of course, everyone was tight in their own bundle. But we spent a long time talking. Getting to know one another.

(She hesitates. There's no response.)

There weren't any curtains there, either. Wouldn't that be a lot better?

(She slowly reaches up to draw back the curtain, but his voice stops her.)

PEDER: Goodnight, Karin. We'll talk in the morning.

(She settles back on her haunches, as the two women again appear in the background, on either side. The older steps forward, her hand shielding a flickering candle.)

OLDER WOMAN: *(whispering to Karin)*

A candle will show you what you want to know!

(She hands it to Karin, passing it close under Karin's face. The younger woman steps over Peder, to slowly draw back the curtain.)

That he's no troll—but a handsome young man!

(Karin moves to see him, faced away from her.)

Lean closer, Karin. To better see his features.

(Karin leans over Peder, studying his face.)

Until the candle drips! So he'll know you've betrayed him!

(Karin cups her hand under the candle too late. The younger woman hisses as three drops fall. Peder wakes, startled by the hot wax, and sits up quickly with a groan.)

PEDER: *(seeing her)*

What have you done!

(Karin drops the candle, falls backwards off the bed.)

OLDER WOMAN: *(exultant)*

She has condemned you, Peder! To marry my daughter!

(The younger woman throws back her shawl, showing her contorted, selfish face. The two women grab hold of Peder's shoulders as he struggles on the bed. The entire canopy and curtains begin to glow bright red, as though the bed were aflame.)

PEDER: *(pleading to Karin)*

If you had waited one year! One year! I'd have been freed from this. I'd have no longer been cursed to be a bear by day and a man by night, but you wouldn't listen! Now all ties are snapt—and I'm to be taken from you—forever!

(He appears to be dragged deeper into the fire, towards the rear of the bed, by the younger woman.)

KARIN: No! Where are you taking him?

OLDER WOMAN: To a castle. East of the Sun and West of the Moon. Where the only wife he'll have...is a Troll Princess. Farewell, Karin.

(She disappears, following Peder and her daughter, the Troll Princess. Karin collapses on the floor in tears as the bedchamber and castle also disappear from view.)

Act Two

Karin is discovered alone and asleep, in the mountain wilderness. Her bundle is beside her, but the castle is gone.

KARIN: *(sitting up)*

Everything's gone. The castle, the courtyard, . . .all those beautiful dresses. And here I am, asleep on the hard-frozen snow. I don't even know where I am.

(She gets to her feet, stiffly.)

Ohhh. I'm chilled to the bone—like an icicle! I'd better move around. Where could it all have gone? Not so much as a step or a stone. But worst of all is...Peder's gone with it. What do I care for him?—If he'd told me the truth....Still, I can't say it wasn't my fault. And I can't say...I don't wish he was here. It's not like he was nice to me...although he did trust me. As much as he could. I'm just feeling guilty!...I wish I could find him.

(An old hag has appeared in the background, hiding from Karin and eavesdropping.)

I wish I could find anyone. I'd better move around or I'll freeze to the spot. Just like a silly little snowman. Well, one good thing. At least I still have my things from home.

(She picks up her bundle as the hag comes forward.)

FIRST HAG: What's in it for me?

KARIN: *(startled)*
What?

FIRST HAG: You heard me! What's in that bundle?

KARIN: Everything I own in the world.

FIRST HAG: I want it.

KARIN: Well, I won't give it to you. What would be left for me?

FIRST HAG: You ought to have had that young man.

KARIN: How did you know. . .?
(She stops, not wishing to say anything to the old woman.)

FIRST HAG: *(smiling)*
We have our ways in the wilderness.

KARIN: Well, . . .whatever you heard—or think you heard—isn't true.

FIRST HAG: What're you doing out here then?

KARIN: *(sullenly)*
Catching a cold.

FIRST HAG: You need help. Help isn't free.

KARIN: Can you help me?

FIRST HAG: Give me the cheese.
(Karin hesitates, then hands her the cheese.)
I know what is in your heart and in the heart of the young man. But you should look for a warmer climate.

KARIN: But I want to find Peder!

FIRST HAG: *(moving away)*
For that, you must ask the next one.

SECOND HAG: *(appearing suddenly)*
   Who me?

KARIN: Who are you?

SECOND HAG: Don't know.
   (Stops to think, comes to a realization.)
   Hunger!

KARIN: You...are hunger?

SECOND HAG: A large part of me is. Do you have food?

KARIN: I gave the other...lady...my only cheese.

SECOND HAG: *(pointedly)*
   So that leaves the bread.
   (Karin tears off half, concealed, gives half.)
   What about the other half? Come on, be quick, my stomach's shrinking!
   (She gives the bread to the hag, who sniffs it, grunting in approval. She begins eating.)

KARIN: Now will you help me?

SECOND HAG: *(between bites)*
   How?

KARIN: Tell me how to get to Peder.

SECOND HAG: I know what is in your heart and in the heart of the young man. But I don't know the way a bit better than the other. Seek safety!

KARIN: I don't care about safety!

SECOND HAG: *(moving away)*
   Then try somewhere else.

KARIN: *(calling after her)*
   Where?

THIRD HAG: *(stepping forward slowly)*
   You might start here.

KARIN: Can you tell me how to find Peder?

THIRD HAG: So many questions you have. What may I ask of you?
   (Pause.)

KARIN: *(unwrapping the bundle)*
   All I have left is this wedding gown. You might as well take it. I've given everything else away.

THIRD HAG: I'll take only the pearls on its hem and sleeves. And for those I'll tell you what you already know. May I have them? Remember their value.
   (Slight pause; Karin tears the hem and sleeves from the gown, giving them to the old woman.)
   Thank you. He is held in a castle, east of the sun, and west of the moon, where only trolls are wont to see him.

KARIN: How can I get there?

THIRD HAG: You have been kind to me. I will be kind to you. And tell that you cannot reach the castle,—

KARIN: What?

THIRD HAG: —that you would be better to give up this journey, and return to your home, where you'll forget that young man.

KARIN: I can't go home! And I'll never forget him!

THIRD HAG: Then your trip will be much harder.
   (The other two hags return, and all three move towards Karin.)

THE THREE HAGS: We know what is in your heart and in the heart of the young man. And for the gifts that you gave us, we give you this one:

THIRD HAG: *(holding a handkerchief)*
   A gentle lace hanky, with two simple jobs.

FIRST HAG: It will show the true nature of those who would own it,—

SECOND HAG: —and covers the worst part of any who hold it.

KARIN: How can that help me?

THIRD HAG: It can't.

FIRST and SECOND HAGS: Nothing can.

THE THREE HAGS: But it may give you time—

THIRD HAG: —to help **yourself.**

KARIN: *(as the hags begin moving away)*
How do I find the castle?

FIRST HAG: *(disappearing from sight)*
You'll find him.

SECOND HAG: *(disappearing)*
When you want to.

THIRD HAG: But this new destination. . .will take an old path.

(The last hag disappears from view, leaving Karin alone again. Pause; she reacts to the chill weather around her and gets her things together to leave.)

KARIN: I'm so cold. Maybe I'd do better. . .to rest a little before I went on.

(The wind can be heard blowing, and Karin pulls her clothes around her more tightly.)

It couldn't hurt. Just to lie down. It might be. . .comforting. For a moment.

(Karin lies down, using her bundle as a pillow for her head. The wind dies down, but a distant voice replaces it.)

VOICE: Karin, . . .

KARIN: *(not wanting to move)*
Yes?

VOICE: Karin, . . .

KARIN: *(looking around)*
   Who is it?

VOICE: Karin, . . .
   (Her mother appears, but she is draped in a shimmering shroud, like an apparition.)
   You've come back.

KARIN: Mother? It can't be, I can't be home.

MOTHER: *(moving towards her)*
   Come closer. Till I embrace you.

KARIN: *(sitting up)*
   Is it really you?

MOTHER: Dear Karin. You look so tired.

KARIN: *(closing her eyes again)*
   I feel tired.

MOTHER: I'll smooth your hair, with this golden comb. It will make your hair longer and lovelier—just as I did when you were younger.

KARIN: *(eyes closed)*
   Did you comb my hair?

MOTHER: You were a baby. You don't remember.

KARIN: *(eyes closed)*
   Your fingers. Cold as fire.

MOTHER: You're chill from your journey. How well to be home.

KARIN: How's Father? Is he. . .better now?

MOTHER: *(combing Karin's hair languidly)*
   Much better. Long past caring.
   (A male apparition appears, in a dark hooded robe. It remains separate from Karin, calling to her.)

FATHER: *(in a weak voice)*
   Karin?

KARIN: *(opening her eyes)*
   Father? Are you here too?

MOTHER: *(combing Karin's hair)*
   Where else would we be, but with you?

FATHER: My darling daughter. . . .

KARIN: Ohhh! No so hard, Mother.

FATHER: *(moving slowly closer)*
   Don't you recognize me?

MOTHER: Of course he was sick after you left.

KARIN: No, Mother, you must've forgotten. He was sick when I left, that's why I—Ow!
   (Mother has again pulled Karin's hair, and continues combing.)

FATHER: *(moving slowly closer)*
   Well, you won't go away now.

MOTHER: *(combing)*
   You'll be safe here at home.

FATHER: *(moving closer)*
   You'll be my tonic.

KARIN: Ow! Please be more careful.
   (To Father, still moving slowly, closing the distance.)
   I wish I **could** stay—Ow!—But I have to free Peder!
   (She pulls free from her mother.)

MOTHER: *(moving after her)*
   Haven't you hurt him enough already?

FATHER: *(beside Karin)*
>You'll stay here forever. Give your father a kiss.

KARIN: *(whispering, as she sees)*
>Mother! He doesn't have any face.

MOTHER: *(moving up behind her to comb)*
>I know. He's much happier.
>
>*(As the mother begins to pull at Karin's hair, the father reaches out to embrace her, exposing a skeletal hand in the long sleeve of the robe.)*

KARIN: *(breaking away, grabbing the comb)*
>Stop it! I have to go!

FATHER: That's right! Run away again!

KARIN: I didn't run away.

MOTHER: Always thinking of yourself!

KARIN: I'm not! I'm thinking of Peder.

MOTHER: What's he to you, compared to your family!

BOTH APPARITIONS: *(closing in on Karin)*
>Come home to us, Karin! Home to us! Home!
>
>*(She rushes between them and past them.)*

KARIN: *(not facing them)*
>No! I have to go on!
>
>*(A sudden powerful wind is heard blowing, and the apparitions disappear under the force of it. The wind suddenly dies down. Karin turns to see they are gone.)*
>
>They've gone. If they were ever here.
>
>*(Karin looks at the comb in her hand, pulls it through her hair curiously, with similar result.)*
>
>Ow!
>
>*(The wind again blows briefly, but mixed in with it is the sound of laughter.)*
>
>Where did that wind come from?

VOICE OF THE EAST WIND: Where does any wind come from? A hole in the wall, or a knot in a tree—I should know, I've squeezed through almost everything.

(The face of the East Wind appears out of an old gnarled tree stump.) You see? There aren't any walls out here, and the closest thing to a tree is this old stump. So that's where you'll find me.

(The face disappears impishly amid the twist of dead limbs and the heavy stump.)

KARIN: I wasn't looking for you.

EAST WIND: *(reappearing in another part of tree.)* I know. You're hunting the White Bear. But you came to the wrong stump for him—you should look in a fir tree.

(He laughs loudly at his joke.)

KARIN: That's. . .very funny.

EAST WIND: Yes, you'll find I'm a—dry wind. Ordinarily of course I'm a flurry of motion; I blow across land, through hill and through dale, and if I find a moment to rest—I know it's a windfall!

(He laughs again, louder than the first time.) Now the westerly wind, he's entirely different—not the least bit breezy like me. He comes from the sea, with rain and with sleet; it makes him something of a wet blanket, if you get my drift!

(He laughs uproariously at his humor.)

KARIN: Can't you be serious?

EAST WIND: I could—but what fun would that be? Wouldn't you rather laugh, and forget your troubles?

KARIN: I'd rather find the troll castle.

(Pause.)

EAST WIND: That's a long ways, and I'm a bit winded. . . .Sorry. Anyway, I can't get you there alone. I'm only one of four winds, you know—I'd need some help.

KARIN: Would the West Wind be willing?

WEST WIND: He might. If you give him good reason.
(The West Wind rises up from a creek bed.)

KARIN: I have to free Peder.

WEST WIND: What makes you think he wants to be freed?

KARIN: He's being held by the trolls. If I don't free him, he'll have to marry one.

WEST WIND: So? Trolls aren't so bad.

EAST WIND: They're kind of cute. In an oily sort of way.
(Both winds nod and laugh, agreeing.)

KARIN: You won't take me?

WEST WIND: There's no need. Things will be fine,—

EAST WIND: Rivers'll flow, winds will blow—

WEST WIND: —if you just leave well enough alone.
(Slight pause.)
Isn't that easier?

KARIN: *(turning to leave)*
I'll find the castle. With or without you.

VOICE OF THE SOUTH WIND: You won't find it with them. That's for sure!
(A large boulder cracks volubly, and from its center rises the South Wind, in the form of a geyser of fire.)
Because neither of them have ever been there!

KARIN: *(to the other two)*
Which one is that?

WEST WIND: *(whispering)*
The South Wind. From a warmer climate.

EAST WIND: *(whispering)*
   Decidedly hot tempered!

SOUTH WIND: With...good...cause,..too! People are always interfering where they're not needed. And usually for selfish reasons!

KARIN: That's not true!

SOUTH WIND: Then why're you going? Hoping to win him back—and his riches too!

KARIN: That's not important! Do you think I'd bother, just for money? I'm going because I care about Peder. I mean,...I care what he thinks about me.
   (She starts to run out.)

SOUTH WIND: *(calling to stop her)*
   Calm down. The trip's too big!

EAST WIND: It's east of the sun and west of the moon—and that's farther than either east or west has been.

SOUTH WIND: Even with all my blustering about I've never been there!

WEST WIND: You might as well spit in the ocean as expect us to take you.

KARIN: Is there any one who can?
   (Pause. They look at one another. From behind them stands the North Wind. He is larger and more majestic than the others.)

EAST WIND: *(whispering)*
   Maybe he can. Compared to his blast, we're nothing but puffs of air.
   (Karin slowly approaches the imposing figure.)

NORTH WIND: I've heard all your answers and I'm satisfied. But you wish to go farther than any of us could take you unaided. I myself have only been there once. And that was to carry an aspenleaf. A full-grown girl is another matter.

KARIN: But I must get there. I have to save him.

NORTH WIND: I know you do. And I agree.

(Addressing the full convocation of winds.)

I propose we all take you there. For once the winds of the north and south, east and west, will join together, and deliver you there on a cushion of cloud.

(Taking her hand, the North Wind prepares her for the trip.)

It will be the softest trek you've ever made.

(The four winds position themselves around her, preparing to carry her on the cloud cover.)

Together, Brother Winds! We've a long journey ahead of us!

(The winds exit, with Karin aloft.)

Scene Seven
Act Three

Karin, carried by the four winds, approaches the Troll Castle.

NORTH WIND: There it is.

(Karin is lowered to the ground, and the other three winds depart.)

We can take you no farther.

KARIN: It's so bright here. How, if the sun never shines?

NORTH WIND: You've entered into a land of mist, far from your world of light to the south. Everything gleams, glittering snow, alluring as gems, in their crystal glow—but they'll freeze you if you stay too long!

KARIN: What can I do?

NORTH WIND: Trapped in those walls are warm hearts. Touch them—and they may help you. But they're gripped by a troll spell, as cold as a fist of ice. Be careful, Karin.

(The North Wind exits. Karin goes towards the castle cautiously, studying it. The younger woman—now clearly seen to be the Troll Princess—enters, spying Karin.)

TROLL PRINCESS: *(haughtily)*
    Who. . .are you? And what. . .are you doing?
    (Without turning to face her, Karin covers her face and disguises her voice.)

KARIN: Pardon me. I was sent to. . .freshen up the place.

TROLL PRINCESS: Ah! For the wedding, no doubt. I'm to be married tomorrow.
    (Karin glances at her.)
    But you don't look like a cleaning troll.

KARIN: *(averting her gaze, whispering)*
    And you don't look like a blushing young bride.

TROLL PRINCESS: What did you say?

KARIN: *(in her distorted voice)*
    Nothing. I'd better get started. Where shall I—
    (She gasps as she sees Peder, dressed in the tallow-stained shirt, led in on the arm of the Troll Queen, and followed by an accompanying troll. They stroll through with the trolls smiling, and Peder apparently asleep.)
    Peder. . . .

TROLL PRINCESS: *(as Peder and trolls exit)*
    Yes. Isn't he handsome?

KARIN: *(in her own voice, letting down her guard)*
    What's wrong with him? He went by without noticing anything.

TROLL PRINCESS: There's nothing wrong with him; he's overcome with happiness. That's my husband-to-
    (She stops.)
    Wait one little niggling moment. How did you know his—
    (Seeing Karin for who she is.)
    Why you little twit! Thought you could creep in here, did you, and disrupt the happy occasion? Well, it's a good thing my mother didn't see you. She'd have turned you into jelly—faster than a toad blinks!

KARIN: And now you're going to tell her, aren't you?

TROLL PRINCESS: No, I'm not, Miss Clever-britches. In fact, I knew who you were before. I'd just decided to keep it a secret.

KARIN: Why?

TROLL PRINCESS: Because it amused me. There you were, trying to fool me—and doing so badly at it! It was...funny! Especially when I was such a convincing ac-ter-ess.

KARIN: Oh, you were! I believed you were just what you seemed to be, every second.

TROLL PRINCESS: *(flattered)*
You did?

KARIN: Yes. I even believed your nose was that impossibly long.

(Stepping closer.)
But wait! In this light your nose looks even longer! So long it could be the snout on a—

TROLL PRINCESS: That'll be enough of that, Miss Sweetness-and-light. You've got some cleaning to do.
(Producing a large black plume.)
Here's a feather from the tail of a great black bird.
(She continues, teasing Karin with obvious enjoyment.)
You'll use it to dust every inch of this place. And as you drag it across these well-turned stones, you'll hear their spirits scream. That should be fun.

KARIN: You're letting me stay.

TROLL PRINCESS: Of course. You'll stay here a good long while. Because when you're done with your dusting...you'll be changed to stone. Like all Christian travellers who fall to this castle, you'll soon become part of it.

KARIN: All right.
(She begins to cry quietly, against her will.)

TROLL PRINCESS: *(agitated)*
Stop that. You can't cry here. It's dangerous! Someone might hear you.

KARIN: *(sniffling)*
Who can hear me now—except trolls? And why should they care?

TROLL PRINCESS: Never you mind, Miss Ten-thousand-questions. Stop it now—or you'll be squeezing tears from a rock!

KARIN: And I'll be the rock!
(As she starts to cry more heavily, she takes out the handkerchief given her by the hags.)

TROLL PRINCESS: Where did you get that!

KARIN: This hanky?
(Troll Princess nods impatiently.)
It was given to me.

TROLL PRINCESS: Well! One good deed deserves another...Give it to me!

KARIN: I couldn't.

TROLL PRINCESS: Why not?

KARIN: It's special.

TROLL PRINCESS: In what way?
(Pause.)

KARIN: *(carefully)*
It brings out the...beauty...of anyone who carries it.
(Pause.)

TROLL PRINCESS: Then I shall wear it at my bosom, and reveal my natural modesty.
(Holding out her hand.)
Hand it over.
(When Karin doesn't, she stomps her feet.)
I want it! And mean to have it! So give it over! Before I burst!

KARIN: If I give it to you, . . .will you let me talk to Peder for one hour?

TROLL PRINCESS: He may not wish to speak to you. After all, he is thinking of his wedding.

KARIN: *(holding out the handkerchief)*
I'll take that chance.

TROLL PRINCESS: Wonderful.
(She snatches it away quickly. Slight pause.)
Go through there. And the stones will whisper the way.
(She smiles at Karin, then turns away to admire the handkerchief. Karin very quickly exits.)
It will make me more beautiful, hmm?
(As she had said, the Troll Princess primly tucks the handkerchief into her bodice, draping it down over her blouse. Seemingly by itself, the handkerchief flies up to cover the Troll Princess' face.)
Oh!
(She struggles with the hanky as the lights fade out on her and up on Peder's chamber.)

Scene Eight

Karin enters the dim chamber where Peder sleeps. Above the doorway are two small stone gargoyles; also in the room are two figures of stone, either columns or other architecture.

KARIN: *(quietly)*
Hello?
(There is a very low growling noise.)
Peder?
(The growling is heard again. Karin looks around the door area, and finally looks at the gargoyles. The growling is heard a third time.)
Is that coming from you?
(She reaches out her hand, and one gargoyle barks and snaps at her. She jumps back, startled, and begins to explore the rest of the room, calling quietly.)
Can anyone hear me?

(She sees Peder asleep on a heavy rug.)

Oh, Peder, I've finally found you. Small voices told me which turns to take, but I wasn't sure whether to believe them. I. . . .

(Peder remains still, even when she shakes him. She stops when he doesn't wake.)

Peder? . . . .Peder!

(She places her head against his chest.)

You're breathing, but so faintly. As though in a deep, deep sleep. . . .I have to talk to you, Peder, to explain. I'm not as bad as you think. I. . .was only curious, that's all.

(Slight pause.)

You can't even hear me. How could you possibly forgive me.?

(She starts to cry, dropping her head on his chest.)

FIRST FIGURE IN STONE: She's upset.

(Pause. Karin doesn't hear them.)

SECOND FIGURE: She's asleep.

(Slight pause. Neither of them moves.)

FIRST FIGURE: I wish we could help.

(Slight pause.)

SECOND FIGURE: Yes. But what can stone do?

(Slight pause. Lights slowly fade in the chamber.)

Scene Nine

The troll attendant enters the chamber, whistling cheerfully. He carries a small platter of raw food and bones.

HORICK: *(to the gargoyles)*

Time for your midnight feeding. Ah ha, I found you napping, didn't I? Is that how you do your job?

(Picking pieces from the platter.)

One bone to Ferd, and one bone to Fjord. And a nice big bone for poor Horick, before he wastes away to nothing.

(He drops one in his own mouth.)

Chew them up soundly.

(All three make loud chomping sounds.)

Good gargoyles.

(He sees Karin, and almost chokes on his bone. He pounds himself on the chest, walks over to the two sleeping figures.)

Seems our prince has a visitor.

(The troll lifts Karin ungracefully, without waking her, and carries her into the other part of the castle. He drops Karin on the ground, waking her, and steps back, leaving Karin on the ground with the Troll Princess standing over her.)

TROLL PRINCESS: You fooled me!

(Karin quickly stands to face the trolls, and tries to appear calm.)

KARIN: What do you mean?

TROLL PRINCESS: *(tossing the handkerchief at her)*

> I mean, I don't appreciate your sense of humor—or your comical handkerchief, which I now return. I hope it works as well for you as it did for me!

KARIN: I don't know what you're talking about. I wasn't even here.

TROLL PRINCESS: I could tell: The flagstones still need dusting. But! . . .perhaps I'll overlook the dust—and simply add a new stone!

KARIN: Wait. Before you do that, I have another gift—one you might like better.

TROLL PRINCESS: I couldn't like it any **worse**. What is it?

KARIN: A golden comb.

(She holds it up. The troll gasps at its beauty.)

> As you brush, it will pull your hair gently, making it longer and lovelier.

TROLL PRINCESS: Oh, I **want** it!

KARIN: *(pulling it back)*

> It's not for sale for gold or money. But I'll let you have it, if you fulfill your end of our deal.

TROLL PRINCESS: What deal?

KARIN: Letting me spend an hour beside Peder.

TROLL PRINCESS: You've already done it.

KARIN: My time wasn't up.

(Pause.)

TROLL PRINCESS: I could take it away from you. However, if that's all you want for it, why should I muss my hands on you. As far as I'm concerned, you can spend all night there—as long as I get the comb.

(Karin hands her the comb. She snatches it quickly, smiling. Indicating the exit.)

Right through there.

KARIN: I remember the way.

(She exits.)

TROLL PRINCESS: *(enticingly)*

Horick? Comb my hair.

(The troll does so.)

Not so hard....That's better....Is it getting longer and lovelier.

TROLL *(nodding as he continues)*

Very much; very much.

(He holds up a handful of hair that has fallen out.)

But what shall I do with it?

(She takes the hair from him, staring at it, then screams and runs off, carrying the hair.)

Scene Ten

Karin peeks in to the chamber, where Peder is still sleeping. When certain no one is there, she runs to his side.

KARIN: *(whispering)*

I may not have much time.

FIRST FIGURE: *(quietly)*
> Caution, Karin.

KARIN: *(whispering)*
> They may come looking for me, once she realizes. Until then, . . .

SECOND FIGURE: *(quietly)*
> We can't move to help you.

FIRST FIGURE: *(quietly)*
> We'll still try to warn you.

KARIN: *(whispering)*
> I want to say I'm sorry. I just wish you could hear me. If there were some way you could show me you'd heard,—

BOTH FIGURES: Footsteps. Down the hall.
> *(Karin stops at the sound of the footsteps, runs back against the wall next to one stone figure. Horick pokes his head into the room, satisfying himself that Peder is alone. The troll exits. Karin steps out from her hiding place.)*

KARIN: *(in her normal voice)*
> Peder? If there were just some way—
>
> *(Her talking alerts the two gargoyles, who begin barking loudly, in high, shrill voices.)*
>
> No! Please be quiet.
>
> *(They continue until Horick returns. He grabs Karin's wrists, and drags her out of the room.)*
>
> I wasn't finished!
>
> *(They both disappear. Slight pause.)*

SECOND FIGURE: I could feel her breathing against me. And crying.
> *(The two stone figures slowly turn to face one another; these are their first movements.)*

Scene Eleven

Karin is thrown into the area where the Troll Princess waits for her. Horick stands over her, but the Troll Princess signals him to go.

TROLL PRINCESS: Do you like this beautiful crown?...It covers my balding head! I look like a snow-vulture, thanks to you!... However,...I'm not going to be angry. No, no. I will very calmly...twist you inside out...and then I'll change you into a stone!

KARIN: *(slowly getting to her feet)*
Before you take my life,...I do have...one more gift to give.

TROLL PRINCESS: I've had enough of your—gifts,—Miss Spiteful-trickery. I want to see you suffer.

KARIN: But you wanted this one.
(She holds up the bedraggled bundle.)
And now you can have it.
(Slight pause.)
My wedding dress. It's the only thing I have left.
(Troll Princess eyes her; pause.)

TROLL PRINCESS: What's wrong with it?

KARIN: Nothing. I just won't be needing it...now.

TROLL PRINCESS: That's true. There won't be any churchbells or cow bells for you, will there?
(Suddenly suspicious.)
What do you want for it?

KARIN: The same as before. To finish the hour as I started it: sitting beside Peder.

TROLL PRINCESS: You don't give up.

KARIN: It's my fault he's here. I owe it to him.
(Pause.)

TROLL PRINCESS: It was pretty, wasn't it?

KARIN: As pretty as the work of ten maiden's hands.

(Slight pause.)

TROLL PRINCESS: All right. I'll take it.

(She slowly reaches out her hands, then snatches it from Karin.)

TROLL PRINCESS: *(continued)*
And what's more, I'll even let you live—at least through the morning. So you can see me wearing it.

(To the troll:)

Take her down to. . .my husband's chamber.

(Horick exits with Karin. When they're gone, the Troll Princess fingers the bundle, tempted to unwrap it. She stops herself.)

No, it would be bad luck to peek. We'll wait till tomorrow. Then we'll show her what a real princess looks like.

(She smiles, exiting with the bundle.)

Scene Twelve

Karin is in the chamber, shaking Peder without any luck.

KARIN: Oh! I've done everything I can, but he won't wake up. Peder! Can you hear me at all? Somewhere inside that sleeping head, is any of this reaching you? . . .I might as well give up now. Let them turn me to stone, or anything else she wants. I couldn't bear to see the wedding. . . .You look so calm. I hope you'll be happy. Oh, Peder!

(She begins to cry, with frustration.)

I tried everything I could. Everything. For you.

(Karin turns to leave. As she moves near the door, the first figure in stone raises its hand to stop her.)

FIRST FIGURE: Karin. . . .

(She jumps back, startled.)

SECOND FIGURE: Not. . .yet. . .

KARIN: You can talk?

FIRST FIGURE: You've heard us before.

SECOND FIGURE: We led you here.

KARIN: Are you. . .statues?

FIRST FIGURE: Yes. Of sorts.

SECOND FIGURE: We're the spirits of unfortunate visitors to this castle. There are many of us here, throughout these halls.

FIRST FIGURE: Trapped in stone. Unable to move. Until you came.

KARIN: How did I help?

SECOND FIGURE: You touched us.

FIRST FIGURE: With your tears.

SECOND FIGURE: Waking our hearts.

KARIN: *(looking back at Peder)*
I wish I could wake him as easily.

SECOND FIGURE: You won't. Not with tears.

FIRST FIGURE: But you can with something else.

SECOND FIGURE: Resting between those two stone gargoyles is a bottle. Each morning he's given a sip of its contents, and it revives him a little. A full drink—

(Without hesitation Karin reaches for the bottle, but one of the gargoyles snaps at her, growling.)

KARIN: It tried to bite me!

FIRST FIGURE: That's their job.

SECOND FIGURE: They may find stone a tougher meal to swallow.

(They reach up, each gripping one of the gargoyles around the muzzle. Karin grabs the bottle, carries it back to Peder. She holds his head up to help him drink. Then she waits expectantly, until he moves.)

KARIN: Peder! I've been waiting all night to tell you—

PEDER: I know. I heard everything you said, though I made no sign of it.

KARIN: Then you know it's too late. Tomorrow you'll be married and I. . . .What can we do, Peder? It's hopeless.

PEDER: If you felt it was hopeless, why did you come back, time and again, to this chamber?

(Slight pause.)

KARIN: To be beside you. That's all. To try and keep my promise. After I'd let you down:

PEDER: You never let me down.

(Karin rests her head against his chest. Slight pause.)

PEDER: *(continuing)*
Everything that happened was because of my own mistake, not because of you.

(Karin tries to stop him, but he continues.)

I was young and clever. I wanted wealth, rich garments—**those** were important. . . .But this was before I'd met you.

KARIN: Do you mean that?

PEDER: I'm happy we met. And I'm glad you came. Whatever the trolls do to me, it'll have been worth it.

(They embrace.)

KARIN: *(noticing)*
You're still wearing this shirt. With the candle-wax.

PEDER: As a reminder. The shirt was the first gift they gave me. I don't seem to be able to get rid of it.

KARIN: Shall I try to clean it?

PEDER: No, not yet. Leave it just as it is. It may be one reason there's still hope.

(Peder has helped her to her feet, and leads her quickly out.)

KARIN: *(stopping at the figures)*
   Wait; what about them?

SECOND FIGURE: There's nothing you can do for us.

FIRST FIGURE: Not until the trolls are gone.

PEDER: Let's go. We don't want to be late.
   (He leads her out of the chamber.)

FIRST FIGURE: Don't worry, Karin.

SECOND FIGURE: Be present at the wedding.

BOTH FIGURES: Then wait. And see.

Scene Thirteen

The Troll Queen and Horick, the troll attendant, are waiting for the wedding.

HORICK: She was just beginning to dress.

TROLL PRINCESS: *(from inside the castle)*
   AAAHHH!
   (She appears, holding the gown.)
   She's done it again! **Look** at this!
   (The gown is piecemeal from having the hem and sleeves torn off earlier.)

TROLL QUEEN: Who's done what, dear?

TROLL PRINCESS: The little twit! She made a fool of me again!
   (She begins to sob.)

TROLL QUEEN: *(realizing who she means)*
   What is that girl doing here?

HORICK: I think she came for the wedding.

-50-

TROLL QUEEN: Stop blubbering. You'll just put on the gown I'd asked for.

TROLL PRINCESS: I don't have it. When I got this one, I told them not to make it.

TROLL QUEEN: Why did you do that?

TROLL PRINCESS: Because it was horrid! I wanted this one.
(She begins to cry more loudly.)
Now I'll look so foolish!

TROLL QUEEN: Who's going to see you!?
(Trying to placate her.)
You'll look fine in this dress. Just take off your crown, and try to get ready.

TROLL PRINCESS: *(quietly)*
I can't.

TROLL QUEEN: Can't what?

TROLL PRINCESS: Take off my crown.

TROLL QUEEN: Why not, may I ask?

TROLL QUEEN: *(crying again)*
Because she plucked me! I'm as bald as a vulture!

TROLL QUEEN: She did that?

HORICK: Actually, madam, I think I did it.

TROLL QUEEN: **You** did that!

HORICK: *(quickly, referring to princess)*
But she gave me the comb!

TROLL QUEEN: Why don't you put a handkerchief over your head, as most brides do?

TROLL PRINCESS: I had a hanky from that girl—but all it did was cover my nose!

(She begins wailing much louder than before.)

TROLL QUEEN: It's all right, dear, it's all right, you just need a mother's understanding. . . .

(Suddenly looks uncomfortable.)

Horick? Take care of her.

HORICK: Yes, madam.

(He positions the princess, who has calmed down to a whimper, spits in his palm, and winds up to slap her.)

TROLL QUEEN: **Not like that!**

(He takes out a hanky, wipes her eyes, blows her nose, turns to the queen.)

HORICK: Better, madam?

TROLL QUEEN: Much. Thank you.

(Peder and Karin enter. He carries the tallow-stained shirt instead of wearing it.)

TROLL PRINCESS: *(pointing)*

There she is! Looking as innocent as a cow!

KARIN: Thank you, . . .Ermengarde. Your—nose—is especially stunning this morning.

(Princess resumes her wailing.)

TROLL QUEEN: **Stop that caterwaul!**

(She assumes an immediate queenly attitude.)

Welcome, Peder. And our pleasant. . .guest. What a wonderful—dreary—day. . .for a wedding.

(She smiles beneficently, a picture of cordiality. Horick fumbles quickly to put on costume accoutrements, making him look like a troll version of a bishop.)

Before we begin the ceremony, I'd like to say a few words about this. . .perfect union, however. To explain its importance.

(Horick, disappointed, begins to remove his costume.)

It isn't a matter of man marrying troll. This would be impossible. Man wasn't born with a natural hoof, and it would not really do to tie a tail to his belt, as we've seen in the past. No, this marriage could not take place...unless the man had earned the right. This man did. He wanted wealth and fine clothing, at any cost—

PEDER: I was younger then.

TROLL QUEEN: *(continuing, enjoying herself)*

—And we gave them to him!...With the understanding that he would appear as a bear by day; and that if he could not find someone to live with him one year as a bear,...he would marry my daughter. For this we gave him many gifts! I see you're holding that lovely silken shirt—the symbol of our agreement. How does it feel now?

PEDER: Much heavier.

TROLL QUEEN: Please put it on. You wear it so well.

(She smiles wickedly, then continues.)

Peder, in his greed and selfishness, was truly a prince among men. Now,—and with your help, Karin,—he'll become what he deserves: . . . .a prince among trolls.

(The Queen steps back majestically, and Horick fumbles into his vestments again.)

PEDER: I, also, have a word before we begin.

(Horick wearily removes his costume.)

I appreciate your gifts, and wish to honor you by wearing them. But if this is to be a real wedding, I must ask that we take the wax from this...lovely shirt. So I may wear it as you gave it to me.

(He steps forward to the Princess.)

This may not be a "wifely duty"...but would you do this for me? In the spirit of a...happy marriage?

(The Troll Princess hesitates, then takes the shirt.)

TROLL PRINCESS: I suppose I could. As a "helpmate."

(She laughs coquettishly.)

I'll just...crack it off...with my fingernails.

(She does so.)

Hmmm. There's still a stain underneath. Horick? The washbasin.
(He brings over a large wooden washtub. The Troll Princess begins to scrub the small spot delicately in the washtub.)

PEDER: Problems, dear?

TROLL PRINCESS: *(smiling to him)*
No, no. I'll get it.
(She holds up the shirt. The stain has grown darker.)
Oh. The stain's growing larger.
(She scrubs more diligently.)
And larger!
(She scrubs frantically.)
And larger!
(She stops, holding up the shirt again. It is almost entirely stained.)

PEDER: *(laughing)*
Are you done, dear?

HORICK: *(leaning in to whisper)*
I think you need a different shirt.
(The Troll Princess stands still, staring at the appallingly stained shirt.)

TROLL QUEEN: I believe I should try, darling.

KARIN: *(taunting her)*
Maybe you'd like me to try.

TROLL PRINCESS: *(throwing it into the tub)*
No! You've fooled me somehow!

KARIN: *(moving to the tub with confidence)*
How could I fool you, Ermengarde. It's only a stain.
(The Troll Princess steps back suspiciously as Karin begins to wash the shirt.)
And I think. . .it's beginning. . .to come out.
(She holds up the shirt, silken and unstained. Offering it to him:)
Peder?

TROLL PRINCESS: *(grabbing it from her hands)*
> No, no, no! If I couldn't fix it, nobody will!
> *(She rips the shirt in half.)*

TROLL QUEEN: *(rushing to stop her)*
> **Don't do that!**
> *(As the shirt is ripped, a thunderclap shakes the castle.)*

TROLL PRINCESS: *(looking up at the sky)*
> What's happening?

TROLL QUEEN: *(as wind begins to blow)*
> The mist! It's blowing away!

HORICK: *(beginning to scuttle off)*
> I think we're in trouble!

TROLL QUEEN: *(grabbing the shirt from Princess)*
> This shirt was our strength! Our agreement!

PEDER: *(shouting over the storm)*
> **Thank you for breaking it!**
> *(Sunlight breaks through the mist; as Horick and Princess try to escape, the Troll Queen runs at Peder, her arms outstretched to seize him. All are frozen in place, however, before reaching their respective goals. Pause. Peder approaches the Troll Queen, pulls the shirt from her fingers carefully, then throws it over his head. He and Karin rush to each other, and embrace, as the two Stone Figures, returned to flesh and blood, enter.)*

FIRST FIGURE: *(prayerfully)*
> Stone thou wast; . . .to stone thou returnest.
> *(Peder and Karin, embarrassed by their closeness, and by the presence of the two figures, step away from each other uncertainly.)*

SECOND FIGURE: *(studying the trolls)*
> Solid rock! As hard as their hearts.

FIRST FIGURE: And not a tear will be shed to restore them. They'll stand here, so long as this castle stands—a warning to all who would practice evil.

PEDER: While you are free. To follow your former lives.

FIRST FIGURE: Yes. Thanks to you. And Karin.

KARIN: Where will you go now?

SECOND FIGURE: *(looking to his companion)*
Home, I hope.

FIRST FIGURE: *(with unspoken fear)*
It's been a long time. . . .And it feels strange to walk about.

SECOND FIGURE: *(smiling gently)*
Yes it does.
(He puts an encouraging hand on the other's shoulder.)
But we'll get used to it.
(The First Figure returns the smile, and they both start off resolutely.)

PEDER: And what about you? Will you also head home?

KARIN: Well, I'm not in as great a hurry as they were.
(Both laugh quietly. Karin looks away from Peder, hesitant to face him. Pause.)
Is that what you want me to do?

PEDER: It isn't for me to say. You know your own mind, Karin. I just want you to be happy.
(Pause.)

KARIN: I made a promise. . .to wait out one year. . .with a young man who needed me. If he was still willing, . . .I think I'd like to keep that promise.

PEDER: With the sun shining on it, this castle doesn't look half so frightening.
(He offers her his arm.)
This way, Karin. I'd like to show you around our new home.
(Together they enter into the castle.)

THE END

NOTES

NOTES

NOTES

NOTES

NOTES

NOTES

NOTES